The Wonders of Water

A DISCOVERY SCIENCE Primary Grades Unit

Robert E. Rockwell

Elizabeth A. Sherwood

Robert A. Williams

David A. Winnett

Dale Seymour Publications®

Contributing authors: *Lori Burns, Lela DeToye, Barbara Goldenhersh, Mary Masterson, Ann Scates, Gale Thacker, Kathy Weber, Sharon Winnett, Cathy Wright*

Field-test sites: *Edwardsville, Illinois, Community School; Hillsboro, Illinois, Community School; Bethalto, Illinois, Community School*

Managing Editor: *Catherine Anderson*
Project Editor: *Mali Apple*
Production Coordinator: *Claire Flaherty*
Design Manager: *Jeff Kelly*
Cover and Text Design: *Christy Butterfield*
Cover Illustration: *Ed Taber*
Photographs: *Bill Brinson*
Composition: *Andrea Reider*
Illustrations: *Rachel Gage*

This book is published by Dale Seymour Publications®, an imprint of Addison Wesley Longman, Inc.

The blackline masters in this publication are designed to be used with appropriate duplicating equipment to reproduce copies for classroom use. Dale Seymour Publications® grants permission to classroom teachers to reproduce these masters.

Copyright © 1997 by Dale Seymour Publications®. Printed in the United States of America.

Order number 36839
ISBN 0-201-49661-5

1 2 3 4 5 6 7 8 9 10 - ML - 00 99 98 97 96

CONTENTS

Introduction		1
Discovery Science		7
The Discovery Center		19
Assessment		21
THE ACTIVITIES		25
ACTIVITY 1	The Shapes of Water	27
ACTIVITY 2	Enough Is Enough	31
ACTIVITY 3	Water Levels	35
ACTIVITY 4	Water and a Little More	39
ACTIVITY 5	Stick with Water	42
ACTIVITY 6	How Many Drops Till It Drips?	46
ACTIVITY 7	Which Drop Hangs Around Longest?	50
ACTIVITY 8	Look Closer	53
ACTIVITY 9	Water Clocks	57
ACTIVITY 10	Through Thick and Thin	62
ACTIVITY 11	Will It Freeze?	65
CHECKPOINT ACTIVITY	Shape Changing	69
Discovery Pages		71
Water Clip Art		76

Introduction

A safe, inexpensive material, water is ideal for studying the general characteristics of liquids. The activities in this unit challenge children to discover the properties of water in a fun and thought-provoking atmosphere. Be part of the excitement and receptive to the children's ideas and theories. They need to operationalize the substance we call liquid if they are to later understand the concept that matter exists as solid, liquid, and gas (and plasma, though this discussion is best left to later in their schooling!). What should your students discover about water and other liquids as they engage in the activities in this unit?

Science Concepts

Three main science concepts will be addressed in this unit:

1. Water is the most common liquid on earth.
2. Liquids have no fixed shape but do have a fixed volume.
3. Many different liquids exist in the world.

Water is the most common liquid on earth. Water is everywhere. Almost three-fourths of the earth's surface is water. The presence of abundant quantities of water has allowed most of the planet's organisms to evolve with a very close dependence on water. The human body is over 70 percent water, as are most other organisms.

Liquids have no fixed shape but do have a fixed volume. Liquid is a phase of matter that always occupies a fixed amount of space. Because the molecules in liquids are free to move around, sliding past and rolling over, under, and around each other, fluids can flow freely and fill containers and vessels evenly. The molecules in solids stay fairly fixed in place. Liquids have no shape of their own; instead, they take on the shape of any container that holds them. When liquids are frozen, they become solids.

Many different liquids exist in the world. In addition to water, many common liquids are available for us to study—oils, paints, juices, literally thousands of them. Although exceptions exist, almost any material—even a rock—can become a liquid through the application of enough heat. Have you ever seen a volcano erupt?

The Wonders of Water 1

The activities in the unit are organized to allow continuous development of the science concepts being studied and function best if used in the order presented.

Getting Ready

To complete many of the activities in this unit, you will need to add the following materials to the Discovery Center:

- Supply of water
- Buckets and dishpans
- Paper towels, towels, sponges, and newspaper
- Containers of all sizes and shapes, including soft-drink bottles and similar plastic containers
- Funnels
- Medicine cups *(the 30-ml or 1-oz cups used to dispense medicine)*
- Spoons
- Measuring spoons and cups
- Waxed paper
- Balloons

You will also need chart paper and colored markers on hand for creating Discovery Charts.

Free Discovery

Free Discovery is an opportunity for the children to talk about what they already know or believe about water and to get acquainted with some of the materials they will be working with in the *Wonders of Water* unit.

Free Discovery is observation, exploration, and interaction that proceeds at the children's own pace, a means to support their curiosity about the world around them. It offers them the freedom to explore in a nonthreatening environment, eliminating the fear of getting "wrong" answers. As the children are in control of their actions, the process builds their self-esteem. In this secure and comfortable environment, children are able to fulfill their natural eagerness to search for solutions to their own questions of why, what, how, and when—in their own way.

During this free exploration, the children experience the materials as learning resources. The time they spend investigating on their own may well be some of their most productive and constructive learning time.

Exploratory freedom reigns in Free Discovery, and it can be a difficult time for adults. We are often tempted to step in at this learning phase, intercepting children's natural curiosity with questions and challenges that are adult- rather than child-initiated. Children are often unprepared for such interruption. We must remind ourselves that Free Discovery is a time for the children to explore materials in their own way.

Conducting the Free Discovery Session

Before starting the first activity, create a class Discovery Chart of what the children already know about water. You might ask such questions as, "Are there things water can do that other things can't do? What do we use water for? Where can we find water?" Have them brainstorm all the ways they have used water since they woke up—brushing their teeth, giving water to the dog, rinsing dishes, washing hands. Challenge them to think of as many words as they can to describe water. Keep the chart posted in the room throughout the unit, and from time to time ask the children if they would like to add to it or change any of the information it contains.

Introduce the children to the materials that will be used in the water activities. If any materials require special care, talk about them with the children. Newspapers spread under a bucket or dishpan will absorb the inevitable drips and spills. Keep towels available so the children can clean up easily. You will make things easier for yourself if you provide these and other materials that enable the children to manage the Discovery Center on their own.

During Free Discovery, talk informally with the children about their explorations. Ask questions to assess what they are doing and thinking about as they work. Monitor them to be sure investigations are being done safely.

You may want to use this opportunity to apply the Success in Science Inventory (see page 23) to evaluate the children's interest and involvement in science. An informal, direct observation of the manner in which the children approach the challenge of scientific investigation will reveal useful information that you can apply later in your interactions with them.

Additional Resources

You may want to add some of these books to the Discovery Center:

- *Up North at the Cabin* by Martha Wilson Chall (New York: Lothrop, Lee and Shepard Books, 1992) explores memories of family trips including water activities such as swimming, fishing, canoeing, and waterskiing.
- *The Magic School Bus at the Waterworks* by Joanna Cole (New York: Scholastic, 1988) tackles the question of how the water cycle works to supply people with water.
- *Follow the Water from Brook to Ocean* by Arthur Dorros (New York: HarperCollins, 1991) relates how water is constantly changing and in motion, and explores how water is used, how it changes things, and its importance to cleanliness.
- *In the Small, Small Pond* by Denise Fleming (New York: Henry Holt, 1993) introduces children to life in a pond through simple rhyming verse.

- *Box Turtle at Long Pond* by William T. George (New York: Greenwillow Books, 1989) is a story told from a turtle's point of view as he tries to meet his basic needs of water, food, shelter, and safety from predators.

- *Drip Drop* by Sharon Gordon (Mahwah, New Jersey: Troll Associates, 1981) is a story about children wearing different articles of clothing in the rain.

- *Sailing to the Sea* by Mary Claire Helldorfer (New York: Viking Children's Books, 1991) is about a sailing trip a boy and his aunt and uncle take from the river to the sea.

- *Amy Loves the Rain* by Julia Hoban (New York: HarperCollins Children's Books, 1989) offers young children the opportunity to look closely at the familiar sounds and colors of a rainy day.

- *The River* by Gallimard Jeunesse and Laura Bour (New York: Scholastic, 1995) contains simple text and colorful images of wildlife that make it an inviting book for all ages.

- *Comes a Tide* by George-Ella Lyon (New York: Orchard Books/Watts, 1990) is a story about families leaving their homes for higher ground during a flood, and their eventual return home.

- *Ocean Parade* by Patricia MacCarthy (New York: Dial Books for Young Readers, 1990) has 1 to 100 fish of many varieties swimming their way through the pages.

- *Pond and River* by Steve Parker (New York: Knoph Books for Young Readers, 1988) is a wonderful pictorial account of freshwater plants and animals that dwell at the edge of the water, on the surface, and in the mud.

- *Water's Way* by Lisa Westberg Peters (New York: Arcade, 1991) explains to young readers the many forms that water can take—such as fog, rain, puddles, steam, and snow.

- *Rainy Day Rhymes* selected by Gail Radley (Boston: Houghton Mifflin, 1992) contains a wonderful selection of poems for reading to children on rainy days.

- *Oceans* by Seymour Simon (New York: Morrow Junior Books, 1990) is a very readable book that describes why our planet is called the water planet and captures the beauty of our oceans in color photographs.

- *Water* by Su Swallow (Chicago: Franklin Watts, 1990) explores through color photographs many aspects of the diverse liquid that is water.

- *On the Riverbank* by Charles Temple (Boston: Houghton Mifflin, 1992) vividly describes experiences of fishing on a riverbank.

Discovery Science

The Discovery Science program is designed to expose children to much more than science skills and concepts. It gives children the opportunity to explore, experiment, create, and problem solve. It encourages them to refine their use of language as they talk about what they are doing or explain what they have discovered. It allows them to apply their emerging mathematical skills in the meaningful context of exploration. And it provides teachers with a curricular framework that capitalizes on the spirit of excitement for discovery that dwells in the minds of children, young and old.

Children come to the educational setting with diverse backgrounds and experiences. Discovery Science integrates science, mathematics, and literacy in a curriculum that recognizes and builds from this diversity.

Using the Discovery Science Units

Traditional primary grades science programs often try to cover a great deal of information in the short school year. The Discovery Science units for the primary grades explore fewer topics in much greater depth.

Plan on spending about eight to ten weeks on each unit. The time required for each activity depends on how much classroom time the teacher wants to devote to science. There is enough material in each activity—including the Additional Stimulation ideas (which include art, literature, and social studies extensions)—for about a week's worth of exploration, or three to four sessions. At a minimum, each activity will require about an hour, including preparation time.

The flexibility of the Discovery Science program allows you to take one of two approaches to using the units in your science program. You can build your science curriculum around Discovery Science units. The set of four units recommended at each grade level stands alone as a complete science curriculum and represents the domains generally considered important for the primary grades: physical, life, and environmental science. We suggest that you select the four units recommended for your grade level, unless your district has other requirements for the sequence of topics in your science program. For grade 1, the recommended units are *The Mysteries of Light* (physical science),

The Wonders of Water 7

The Wonders of Water (physical science), *You and Your Environment* (environmental science), and *Animals and Their Homes* (life science).

Alternatively, you may choose to supplement or enhance your existing curriculum with a favorite unit or two. Units may be used at one grade higher or lower than the designated level.

Teaching Discovery Science

Discovery Science visualizes children as learners actively constructing knowledge rather than passively taking in information. Through their activity, children *form* knowledge and make it their own.

GOALS FOR PRIMARY GRADES SCIENCE

1. To provide an environment that supports active discovery.

2. To promote the development of fundamental problem-solving skills.

3. To promote personality dispositions indicative of good scientific problem solvers.

4. To promote children's awareness of careers in science, mathematics, and technology.

5. To raise children's comfort and confidence level with science through conscious efforts to counter bias against science.

6. To promote development of a knowledge base of basic scientific principles and laws, the foundation upon which a clear and accurate understanding of the world can develop. A solid foundation reduces the risk of children acquiring misconceptions that may hinder their understanding of more complex science concepts later.

The inquiry model that prevails in Discovery Science begins with asking the children: *What do you know about this topic?* This is followed by Free Discovery, in which the children explore the new materials on their own. Then, they are asked: *What did you learn?* This question is followed by experiences designed to encourage the children to ask questions and to seek their own answers. Through this process, children are *empowered* to become scientists.

To be effective, a science program must emphasize interaction with the environment, natural as well as social. To promote social interaction, the teacher and the children in Discovery Science have specific roles.

THE ROLE OF THE TEACHER

- To encourage children to explore and experiment independently
- To create an atmosphere conducive to learning
- To introduce new ideas, materials, and procedures
- To encourage inquiry and creativity
- To model inquiry, questioning, and problem solving
- To model safe practices
- To provide sufficient materials, information, and space
- To support developmentally appropriate activity
- To assess and evaluate children's learning

THE ROLE OF THE CHILDREN

- To care for and function independently
- To understand that they are in control of their actions
- To feel good about discovery
- To cooperate with other children
- To collect data and document activities
- To explore materials and ideas
- To realize that answers are not right or wrong but simply the result of inquiry
- To communicate their experiences

Discovery Groups

We encourage teachers to have children work in small groups whenever the nature of the activity allows for this type of interaction. We refer to these heterogeneous, collaborative groups as Discovery Groups to reinforce the importance of inquiry and investigation. In some activities, it will be appropriate to assign each child a role within the group, such as Principal Investigator (directs the investigation), Lab Manager (gathers materials and cleans up), Recorder (keeps track of what is discovered), and Reporter (shares the group's findings with the class).

When children work in interactive groups, several exciting things happen. The investigation is enhanced, in that now there are several inquiring minds generating questions and trying to understand the observed phenomena. The skills of observation, classification, and communication take on new importance, as they become the vehicles by which the group travels together in the directions the inquiry takes them. Management of the

The Wonders of Water 9

children and equipment becomes easier, as the teacher has only to deal with several groups rather than many individuals.

Limiting the Number of Concepts Explored

Each unit in the Discovery Science program addresses a relatively few number of science concepts.

Textbooks are often packed full of concepts and terms that children are expected to absorb during the brief school year. For most young learners, this is far too much in too little time. A hurried exposure to science may fail to provide the opportunity for the rich conceptual development that is possible with a more coherent, thoughtful approach that supports quality over quantity. When learning is centered around a small number of core concepts, the learner can spend enough time with the materials and concepts to master them.

Too often, instead of giving children the self-confidence that comes with mastering new ideas or skills, we move them quickly from one topic to the next. We are subtly teaching them to be satisfied with incompetence. With a limited number of topics, children have more opportunities to experience feelings of competence and mastery.

Repetition will reinforce children's awareness of their own competence and the confidence that awareness brings. Materials should be accessible and the curriculum developed in such a way that children can return to or repeat experiences that they may have completed some time ago.

Supporting Emerging Language and Literacy Skills

The Discovery Science program is designed to familiarize children with the process of asking a question and looking for an answer, and it encourages children to devise their own ways to communicate their experiences. As children seek to describe their observations accurately and to share their discoveries, they will improve their use of language and expand their vocabulary. Alternative methods of communication—such as drawings, charts, and graphs—are introduced and used. The language focus should remain on effective communication and interesting and accurate content rather than precise spelling, grammar, and penmanship.

Group experiences model diverse uses of language and literacy and encourage sharing and collaboration, which require meaningful oral and written communication.

Discovery Charts

Discovery Charts, lists of "what we know," are used periodically to record what children know and to give direction to class planning. They communicate to children in a concrete way that what they are doing is important enough to write down and remember. The first Discovery Chart is created at the start of the unit, during Free Discovery, to assess children's current level of understanding. Variations on the basic Discovery Chart are suggested throughout the activities.

Make additions to Discovery Charts whenever significant new information is generated. You may want to add new concepts in a different color. This will help emphasize to children, and to families who see the Discovery Charts on the wall, that more knowledge is being acquired.

Review the Discovery Charts with children often to reinforce the science concepts and to support emerging literacy skills. At times, children may realize that a statement written earlier is inaccurate. For example, an early Discovery Chart may state that "magnets pick up metal," yet the children have since discovered that there are some kinds of metal that magnets will not attract. When children become aware of the discrepancy between an earlier statement and their current knowledge, help them to create a new, more accurate statement.

You may want to revisit the charts with the class later in the year, long after work on a unit is complete, to convey the value and consistency of the information the children have acquired.

Discovery Journals

Discovery Journals are a key component of Discovery Science. They document the children's explorations, serve as a means of communicating to others, and support emerging literacy skills. It is a rewarding experience for children to look back at their entries and see their own progress. The journals are also a permanent record of what the children have learned that they can share with their families.

The children will need a separate Discovery Journal for each unit. An inexpensive three-ring plastic binder is ideal and will last all year. The cover can be labeled *Discovery Science* with a permanent marker, and the children can make title pages for each unit. The binder allows flexibility as the children create their journals, as they can insert drawings and extra pages as needed. When the unit is complete, the pages can be removed and stapled or bound together to form a Discovery Journal for the unit. As an alternative to binders, Discovery Journals may

The Wonders of Water 11

be preassembled, allowing at least one sheet of paper per activity, and stapled together. Children can make and decorate construction-paper covers.

Blackline masters are provided for some of the activities. Use these Discovery Pages whenever you like to supplement the children's Discovery Journal entries or simply to provide one model for how their responses to an activity might be recorded. Keep in mind that other recording methods are always appropriate.

The page of clip art at the back of the book will inspire and help you and your students prepare your own charts and tables. Children may want to affix some of the images to pages of their Discovery Journals to illustrate what they have done and learned.

Making Connections to Other Areas

The activities and associated extension ideas in each unit present many opportunities to connect the science experiences with mathematics, technology, art, and other areas. In addition, several take-home activities are offered as a way to involve the family in what the child is learning at school.

Connections to Mathematics

Measurement and basic arithmetic skills are needed to quantify observations. Science discovery and investigation provide the perfect opportunity for children to apply graphing, charting, and data-analysis skills to real problem-solving situations.

More important, when mathematics is integrated into the science curriculum, children learn science and mathematics skills together as part of a unified curriculum. Showing children the connection of numbers to the practical examples from science enables them to begin to operationalize mathematical skills.

Connections to Language

Discovery Science offers continuous opportunities for written and oral language development. Children are encouraged to share their ideas with the class as Discovery Charts are generated and in their small Discovery Groups as they work through activities. Discovery Journals support clear written communication about observations and speculations.

The Science Vocabulary in each activity is the specialized vocabulary that children must comprehend to fully understand the science concepts they are exploring. We encourage you to work with the children to develop operational definitions of the words that are introduced. The *operational definition* of a word is simply the meaning the children derive that fits with their own ongoing exploration of the concept. We are trying to give children the confidence to explore and discover on their own—to have power over the direction their inquiry follows. Encouraging them to use their own operational definitions will allow them to use language more freely. Misconceptions of word meanings are best resolved through additional experience rather than verbal correction of their understanding.

Connections to the Family

As the child's first caregiver and teacher, parents have both the right and the responsibility to be involved in their child's formal education. Research conducted in a variety of educational settings over the past three decades suggests that parents who establish a learning environment in the home, who stimulate their children's interest in learning, and who support their children's natural curiosity, foster attitudes that help ensure their children's academic achievement. In addition, involved parents develop more positive attitudes toward the school and its goals. (R. E. Rockwell, L. C. Andre, and M. K. Hawley, *Parents and Teachers as Partners: Issues and Challenges.* Fort Worth, Texas: Harcourt Brace College Publishers, 1996)

Families and educators have a common goal: concern for the children. Home and school are both important functional areas for children. Mutual respect and support between home and school is essential for helping children to develop and learn and for creating the most effective learning environment. Early childhood and primary grades programs can encourage parents to be part of the education process. The Discovery Science program provides a natural avenue for children, families, and teachers to work together.

THE ROLE OF THE FAMILY

- To encourage the child's own discovery process
- To model inquiry and problem solving
- To resist answering and solving discovery activities before the child has done so
- To enjoy doing science activities with the child
- To feel free to communicate with the child's teacher, to ask questions, and to seek additional information when needed
- To listen to and give information to the child, and to remember that it is all right for any participant to make mistakes or to say "I don't know"

The Wonders of Water 13

- To share available resources from home, such as junk materials for making things or information and materials related to occupations or hobbies that correspond to the unit topic

Family activities reinforce what the children are learning at school. They empower children by giving them the opportunity to share their knowledge with their families. Each family activity idea is presented in a note that you send home with the children. You may want children to record what they learn at home in their Discovery Journals for sharing with the class later.

Developing Science Process Skills

The success of the Discovery Science approach to learning science will be evident in the children's ability to perform the skills of inquiry, more generally called *science process skills*. Most approaches to encouraging the development of science process skills are aimed at learners who have reached a level of mental development that allows them to reason and understand abstract ideas.

This curriculum takes a *developmental approach* to teaching young children the skills of research and investigation, beginning with the premise that young learners require focus and guidance in the initial steps of acquiring these skills. The Discovery Science program presents the skills in a way that assists young learners in their early efforts with the specific processes.

Activities for this unit have been designed to facilitate this process. For example, if we want children to use their senses to observe certain physical characteristics of the objects they are investigating, we select activities that highlight the desired observations, thus helping them to focus their senses on the relevant observations. More sophisticated science process skills developed in the unit are making inferences and making predictions. Again, specific activities have been developed to provide the teacher with ideal conditions in which to guide the children to making their own inferences and predictions.

Following are descriptions of the science process skills developed in this unit.

Focused Observation

Focused Observation activities allow teacher-directed quality control over the types of observations the children are making. Children are recording these observations in their minds. Later, they can recall an observation and fit it into a larger conceptual framework that allows them to make sense of what they are doing or learning.

Because children will use current observations as a basis on which to build future understanding, you have two major instructional concerns. First, there are observations about each science theme that children need to make; if they are not made, the children will not begin to understand the concepts. Second, children are continually making inferences about what they have observed. Some of these inferences are correct, and some may not be.

Focused Observation activities are designed to direct children's observations to specific aspects of each concept. You will frequently ask the children to organize their observations and to make them more precise. The children will be asked to isolate various factors that affect their subject and to alter them to make new observations regarding the effect these changes have. For example, if the children are rolling a ball down an inclined plane, they may be asked what would happen if they changed the angle of the plane.

Observing to Classify

Encouraging children to make use of their observations reinforces the importance of being a good observer. Classification tasks provide children with an opportunity to make decisions and to be in control. A successfully organized group of objects gives them immediate satisfaction in knowing that the task is over and has been done well—similar to the feeling adults experience when all the pieces of a puzzle fit together.

Organizing and Communicating Observations

Science seeks to find order and structure in our world. Free Discovery, Focused Observation, and Observing to Classify are the initial experiences children need if they are to begin establishing order in their world. Your next task is to encourage them to make meaningful drawings in their Discovery Journals and to create charts and graphs to help them describe their observations. Through this process, they will begin to understand the need for orderly record keeping and systematic analysis of information—as well as the importance of clear communication—at their level, of course. In addition, they will see that much of what they are learning about numbers and simple arithmetic is quite useful in scientific discovery.

Guided Inference

When we make inferences, we are attempting to explain what we have observed. Young learners need guidance to develop this skill; they are still operating at a concrete level of thinking and must be encouraged to explain their thoughts. Moreover, their frame of reference is limited since they have not yet compiled a broad base of knowledge and understanding.

You can guide children in their initial attempts at formulating inferences by setting the stage and coordinating the actors. When you direct children to attempt activities that allow them to observe interesting yet familiar phenomena, and then to explain in their own words why something behaved the way it did, you are guiding their inferences.

Guided Prediction

After experimenting with certain materials, children will be asked to predict how other materials will respond to the same conditions. Your attempts to guide their predictions should begin with simple forecasts of events that have yet to take place. You must make sure their initial predictions are directly related to the frames of reference they have developed during the course of the discovery activity.

Encouraging Family Involvement

In addition to sending home and reviewing the suggested family activities, there are many other steps you can take to involve families in their children's learning experience.

Introducing Discovery Science: A Family Meeting

Invite families to be a part of a Discovery Science hands-on meeting. In the meeting, you will talk with them about the program and how it will be implemented. The major focus of the meeting is to inform families of the emphasis that the Discovery Science curriculum places upon working with parents as partners in the education of their children.

Prepare the Discovery Center to allow families to interact with some of the Discovery Science activities and materials in the same way their children will. Introduce the activities that you will periodically be sending home. During the meeting, you may discover special interests or related skills some family members have and would be willing to share with the class.

After attending the meeting, families will be more adept at supporting, modeling, and discussing Discovery Science with their children.

Discovery Science Newsletter

Create a Discovery Science newsletter, either as a separate piece or as a portion of a general newsletter. In the newsletter, inform families of science-related activities at school and in the community, including field trips, classroom visitors, and great discoveries that will help keep interest and input coming.

Family Letters and Discovery Science Notes

Send a letter home to families at the start of each Discovery Science unit to introduce the topic and to ask for support and ideas for resources. You might mention that the children will periodically be bringing home activities to share with their families, and that any observations or comments families have to offer on these experiences would be quite welcome.

Send home brief notes to update families on current activities, to remind them of an upcoming field trip or event, or to relate their child's recent discovery.

Family Volunteers

Discovery Science can provide opportunities and access for families to get involved, from offering resources and materials to volunteering at the school. Family volunteers can enrich the learning process and expand the learning environment for children as they share their skills, personal expertise, and the enthusiasm of discovery.

The Discovery Center

A well-organized and well-maintained science center offers a central focus for a successful science program. The Discovery Center sets the stage for exploration. It provides ample materials in an accessible way, has safe and orderly workspaces, and serves as a resource and library. The Discovery Center also serves as the storage site for materials to be used elsewhere.

By its very nature, the Discovery Center promotes problem solving and positive risk taking because children work largely on their own. Children learn to make independent decisions as they explore concepts designed to teach the how-to of science rather than words and facts.

The size and organization of your classroom will determine your Discovery Center's total area. When designing your center, consider how many children you would like it to accommodate at one time.

Collecting Materials for the Discovery Center

Materials in the Discovery Center should be sturdy, simple, and easy to handle. If space does not allow for a permanent center, select materials that can be set up quickly and stored easily.

The Discovery Center should contain the following basic equipment:

- safety goggles
- laboratory coats (paint aprons or smocks)
- magnifying devices such as hand lenses, bug boxes, and two-way magnifiers
- double-pan balance with standard and nonstandard units of mass
- standard and nonstandard measuring devices for length and volume
- spoons, scoops, droppers, and forceps
- containers such as bowls, bottles, and cups
- sorting and storage containers such as egg cartons and clear plastic vials with lids
- cardboard or plastic foam food-packaging trays for sorting and mess containment

The Wonders of Water 19

- writing materials
- cleanup equipment such as buckets, sponges, dustpans, and hand brooms

Setting Up the Discovery Center

Storage space must be thoughtfully designed to meet your classroom's instructional needs. Several types of storage are necessary.

The materials listed above should be out and available at all times, promoting their use and encouraging children to find new functions for them. Shelves, tables, and pegboard are useful for this type of storage.

Some materials must be stored out of the way until needed. Plastic storage tubs are an excellent choice: they come in a variety of sizes and stack easily, allowing whole sets of materials to be stored together. The availability of clear lids and a variety of colors increases their flexibility. They can be made accessible to the children or stored out of reach.

Other materials must be available but not necessarily out on shelves. Resealable plastic bags are useful for containing small sets of materials. Small tubs, boxes, and crates are also helpful.

All storage space and containers should be easy to clean and label, inexpensive, and easy for children to use and keep in order. Racks, hooks, shelves, and storage closets should be labeled.

Also consider the following when designing your Discovery Center:

- Clutter-free surfaces for work areas.
- Places on shelves, tables, or the floor to leave materials for an extended time or study.
- Areas should be easy to clean and cleanup materials readily available. Responsibility for accidents, along with normal messes, is part of science training.
- Water should be available either from a sink or special containers. Water in the area means less traffic to the taps in the bathrooms.

Share special care or storage requirements with the children when you introduce them to new materials. Discuss safety rules each time a new material or piece of equipment is added to the Discovery Center. Model safe behavior, and set clear limits to enable children to handle and interact with the materials safely.

Assessment

The assessment and evaluation procedures used in Discovery Science are consistent with sound test and measurement approaches. They have been developed to be practical and informative for the primary classroom setting.

Assessment and evaluation in Discovery Science are closely tied to instruction and are embedded in the learning cycle rather than being "tacked on," as a caboose at the end of the train. Several train engines are spread throughout the line of cars—engines that give power and purpose to the learning activities. When assessment measures are inseparable from the curriculum and the instructional approach, we say they are *authentic*. Discovery Science uses authentic assessment measures in such a way that both teachers and children perceive the assessment as an extension of the learning process.

Be aware of the diversity of the developmental levels of children in your classroom. Nothing in your evaluation should discourage children in the growth of their inquiry skills or, even worse, set their present attitude against scientific inquiry—an attitude they may well possess the rest of their lives. A willingness to think, to explore, and to search for answers is critical for the development of good problem-solving skills.

The assessment system used in Discovery Science has three components: the Success in Science Inventory, curriculum-embedded assessment, and the use of Discovery Charts.

Using the Success in Science Inventory

The Success in Science Inventory (SSI) is a checklist used to record children's dispositions toward scientific inquiry. When certain behaviors or choices are made by a child, we begin to formulate an understanding of the level of interest and enthusiasm that child has for discovery.

Although the SSI may be used at any time in the curriculum, we recommend that it be used during each unit's Free Discovery period to assess the children's interaction with materials in the center and with each other. Evaluate each child in each of the four science dispositions throughout the year. The suggested levels of performance are Not Apparent, Emerging, and Developed. To simplify scoring, scale of 1 to 3 is suggested.

The Wonders of Water 21

Evaluation using the SSI will give you a picture of how the class is progressing overall. You will know that Free Discovery is successful when these early problem-solving behaviors emerge in the children. As you observe their behavior, you will get a feel for when it is time to move on to the next phase of Discovery Science. The children will show that they are ready to do more.

To use the SSI, administer it during the Free Discovery session. You may elect to observe and record dispositions for all children each time or to select certain children at different times. Observe and record children's behavior for each of the four science dispositions, indicating the child's level within a particular disposition. The more marks a child receives, the greater the indication of success in science.

The SSI assesses four science dispositions:

1. The child manipulates objects for useful observations. *Does the child explore new materials placed in the Discovery Center in a thoughtful way?*

2. The child seeks a clear understanding of the questions *who, what, where,* and *when*—the facts. *When observing something unique on a field trip, does the child ask relevant questions?*

3. The child seeks reasons: asks the question *why* and tries to answer it through further exploration. *As the child works on a project that continues to fail, does the child persist in trying alternatives?*

4. The child communicates the results of observations and investigations. *Does the child talk with you or others about Discovery Science activities?*

Using Curriculum-Embedded Assessment

The second assessment instrument used in Discovery Science is curriculum-embedded assessment, which is in several forms.

Assessing the Activity

Assessing the Activity is found at the end of each activity. It is a formative evaluation that provides ongoing information about how successfully the children are mastering skills and understanding concepts. If the children are unable to meet the expectations of the task, you can act immediately to guide them toward better understanding of the concepts. You may want to keep a record of these formative evaluations for each child in individual portfolios.

Success in Science Inventory

Science Dispositions

Child's Name	1	2	3	4	Comments

1. Manipulates objects for useful observations.

2. Seeks a clear understanding of the questions *who, what, where,* and *when*—the facts.

3. Seeks reason. Asks the question *why* and tries to answer it through further explorations.

4. Communicates the results of observations and investigations.

© 1997 Dale Seymour Publications®

The Wonders of Water 23

Checkpoint Activity

The Checkpoint Activity at the end of the unit is a summative look at how well children have developed the desired skills. Although not to be considered a final unit test, the Checkpoint Activity does provide an opportunity for you to observe the children's level of skill mastery. If children have performed well on the Assessing the Activities, they should have little trouble completing the Checkpoint Activity.

Additional Stimulation Activities

The Additional Stimulation ideas suggested in each activity will assist you in expanding the children's newly acquired knowledge and incorporating it into other curricular areas. These mini-activities can also serve to reinforce a science concept when the children have not completely mastered it during the main activity.

Discovery Journals

The single most important thing to remember when you review the children's Discovery Journals is that *they belong to the children*. They are the children's own record of their learning and discovery. Letter grades, happy or sad faces, or comments written on their pages will quickly eliminate the children's spontaneity, their sense of ownership, and the pride and improvement in skill that comes from *self*-assessment.

Using Discovery Charts

When created by the class at the beginning of a unit, Discovery Charts serve as a preassessment. They tell you what the children as a whole already know, and they can make you aware of misconceptions.

When you take the time to refer to an old chart, add to it, or create a new one, the children will see that they are learning. Discovery Charts also can be used as a part of individual assessment, as they contain the main body of knowledge generated by the children themselves. Each child should have an understanding of most if not all of the information the Discovery Charts contain.

The Activities

ACTIVITY 1

The Shapes of Water

Water is the most common liquid on earth and the easiest to obtain and use. When the children discover the characteristics of water, it will be much easier for them to understand the properties of other liquids. Expect a wet and messy time in this activity. Be prepared with towels and newspapers—or move outside!

CONNECTIONS

 TO LANGUAGE

Expressive Language—The children record their observations in their Discovery Journals, making drawings and writing captions as their ability allows.

 TO MATHEMATICS

Volume—The children begin to explore conservation of volume as they pour the same quantity of water into a variety of containers.

Before the Activity

Prepare pitchers of lightly colored water. The coloring will help the children to see the water levels.

What to Do

1. This activity can be done individually, in Discovery Groups, or as a class. Give each child or group a cup of water, and let them pour the water into several different containers. Ask them to observe how the shape of the water changes to match the shape of each container. As they experiment, some children may discover that the volume remains the same even though the shape of the water is changing.

2. Have the children draw some of the shapes they make with their water in their Discovery Journals. They may caption

Science Process Skill

Focused Observation

Science Concept

Liquids have no fixed shape but do have a fixed volume.

Science Vocabulary

H_2O
liquid
shape
shape names
solid
volume
water

Materials

water *(lightly tint the water with food coloring)*

towels

pitchers

cups *(1 per child or group)*

clear containers of various shapes and sizes, including cups, bottles, cartons, old vases, perfume bottles, and plastic bags

balloons and string

funnels

rubber bands

yarn

pipe cleaners *(wrap the sharp ends with tape)*

trays or dishpans

freezer

Activity 1 The Shapes of Water 27

THE CONCEPT OF CONSERVATION

Between the ages of 6 and 8, children begin to construct an understanding of conservation. *Conservation* is the principle that changing the physical attributes of an object (shape, length, direction, position) does not alter the amount of material present (its volume). All children learn about conservation through their experiences and at their own pace. Given ample experience with subdividing masses of clay or other material, they learn about the conservation of substances; experience with similar volumes in different shapes teaches them about the conservation of volume.

their drawings if they choose. You may wish to share with them the chemical symbol for water, H_2O. They might enjoy the novelty of being able to make this new reference to a familiar substance.

3. Help the children use funnels to fill balloons with water (be careful of the water pressure from the faucet—and don't fill the balloons too full!). Tie the balloons closed. Let the children use yarn, string, rubber bands, and pipe cleaners—and anything else they can think of—to change the shape of the balloons. You may want to have them do this activity over a dishpan or on newspaper in case of leaks.

4. When each child has "sculpted" a balloon, place all the balloons in a freezer. Ask, "What do you think will happen to your balloon sculptures?"

5. When the balloons have frozen, return them to the children. Ask them to cut away the balloon and other materials to expose the piece of ice. Talk about the fact that water, a liquid, is now ice, a solid. It now has a definite shape.

6. Ask the children to draw their ice shapes in their Discovery Journals and label them. Ask, "What will happen to the ice when it warms in the air? Will it keep its shape?"

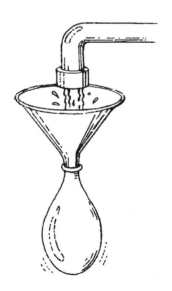

Assessing the Activity

Do the children's journal entries reflect an understanding of the way liquids change shape? Do the children respond in discussion with information that reflects a knowledge of liquids having no definite shape?

28 Discovery Science

Additional Stimulation

What Holds Water?—Bring in several containers of a variety of shapes, some that will hold liquids and some that won't. Oatmeal and cereal boxes, plastic bags, paper bags, cans, bottles, cardboard boxes, sieves, nets, and jars all make wonderful demonstrations. Have the children divide the containers into those that will hold liquid and those that won't. Then, help them test each container. Were any put in the wrong category? Why? Ask the children to list characteristics of a container that can hold a liquid and to talk about how it differs from one that cannot.

Activity 1 **The Shapes of Water** 29

Away It Goes—Have the children each choose a container that they think will hold the water their ice sculpture will produce as it melts. Place the containers in dishpans or trays to catch any overflow. Have the children write and draw about the changes they observe, including whether the water from each sculpture fits the chosen container.

A Roomful of Sculptors—Have the children make a class poster with captioned photographs of their balloon sculptures. They may even want to include photographs of the puddles made by the melted sculptures.

Liquid Poster—Have the children collect pictures of liquids for a poster. They may want to make several posters, classifying liquids by use—such as liquids for food, for cleaning, for work, and for fun.

ACTIVITY 2

Enough Is Enough

In this activity children will continue to explore the idea that water maintains its volume even when its shape changes. They will realize that a bottle of one size will hold the liquid of another bottle of the same size, and that smaller full bottles will only partially fill a larger bottle. These kinds of experiences will support their eventual understanding that water has a definite volume regardless of the shape of its container.

CONNECTIONS

 TO LANGUAGE

Expressive Language—The children use comparative terms when discussing their observations.

Discovery Journals—The children draw their observations in their journals.

 TO MATHEMATICS

Volume—The children continue to explore the concept that the volume of a liquid remains constant regardless of the shape of its container.

Before the Activity

This activity could easily be done as a learning station in the Discovery Center.

Create two bottle pairs for each pair of children or for each Discovery Group, one with bottles of the same size and one with bottles of different sizes. Fill a 1-liter bottle with colored water and connect it to another 1-liter bottle with a pipe connector. Label the pair of bottles with an A. Fill another 1-liter bottle with colored water and connect it to a 2-liter bottle, and label the pair B. Make additional combinations if you like.

Turning a unit upside down will allow the water to bubble into the other container. Rotating the bottle while it is overturned will cause a tornado-like spout or vortex to form and empty the bottle faster; it is a fascinating phenomenon.

Science Process Skill
Focused Observation

Science Concept
Liquids have no fixed shape but do have a fixed volume.

Science Vocabulary
comparative terms such as equal to, the same as, more than, and less than
empty, full, overflow
liquid
liter
volume

Materials
water and towels

clear plastic soft-drink bottles in various sizes, including 1-liter and 2-liter bottles

pipe connectors (cut the bottom from plastic film canisters, or cut a piece of 1-inch-diameter clear plastic pipe into 2- to 2.5-inch lengths)

food coloring

crayons

Activity 2 **Enough Is Enough** 31

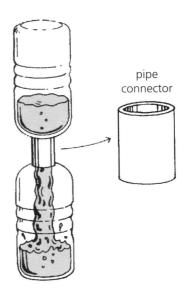

What to Do

1. Show a pair of same-size joined bottles to the children. Ask, "What do you think will happen if I turn this pair of bottles upside down? How much water will there be in each of the bottles?" Talk with them about their ideas.

2. Invert the bottles. Discuss what the children see and how their observations relate to their expectations. Have them draw the pair of bottles in their Discovery Journals as they looked originally and as they looked when the water stopped flowing. Ask, "What do you think will happen every time I turn the bottles over? How much water will be in each bottle?"

3. Repeat the process with a pair of bottles that are of different sizes. The smaller quantity of water will pass into the bigger bottle and back again. Before you invert the bottles, have the children draw how they expect the water to look once you turn the bottles over. Invert the bottles. Ask, "Did what you

32 Discovery Science

MORE ABOUT CONSERVATION

Because the children do not yet fully grasp the concept of conservation of volume, the shape of a container is likely to influence their perception of the volume of water in that container. They will benefit from every opportunity they get to manipulate materials that involve them in exploring the concept of conservation. We can *tell* children that the volume of a liquid remains constant no matter what container it is in, but they won't believe it until they experience it for themselves.

expect to happen actually happen?" Encourage them to use descriptions such as *more than, less than, the same as, half full, empty,* and *overflow.*

4. Let the children work with a partner or in Discovery Groups to manipulate the various bottle pairs and to make their own combinations. One child can set up the bottles, and another can use a crayon to mark on the bottle where they expect the water level to be after the bottles are inverted. Have them draw about what they find in their Discovery Journals.

Assessing the Activity

Do the children express some understanding of the idea that although the water moves from container to container and changes shape, the *amount* of water remains the same?

Pour an equal amount of water into a tall, narrow container and a wider, shorter container that hold the same amount of liquid. Have a child pour water from each container in turn into a measuring cup to measure the amount each holds. Ask, "Does one container hold more water, or do they hold the same amount?" If the child does not realize that the containers

Activity 2 **Enough Is Enough** 33

hold the same amount, he or she has not yet achieved an understanding of conservation of volume. This is a concept that children acquire over time through many experiences with volume comparisons. Explorations throughout the unit will move them closer to this understanding.

Additional Stimulation

Let's Do It Again—Collect plastic containers in various shapes and sizes and match them according to the size of their openings. Fill one of a matched pair with colored water, and attach it to the other container with duct tape. Place the sets in the Discovery Center. The children can work in pairs, predicting the change in water level when each pair of containers is inverted.

Beginnings with Ratios—With your help, the children may begin to develop some understanding of the proportional relationships between two bottles. For instance, the ratio of the volume of a 1-liter bottle to a 2-liter bottle is 1 to 2.

Volume Words—With the children, make a list of words that describe changes in volume, such as *full, overflowing, half full, half empty,* and *equal to.* The children can make drawings to illustrate the words.

Look at It Sideways—Ask, "What happens when the bottle pairs are laid on their sides? If the smaller bottle is full, will the water flow into the larger bottle? What if the larger bottle is full?" Let the children play with these ideas and share their discoveries.

ACTIVITY 3

Water Levels

This activity offers the children more experience with the concept that although the shape of the container holding a liquid may change, the liquid's volume remains the same. The children will make predictions as they group containers by expected volume. With practice, most children will become fairly adept at determining which containers will hold a given amount of water.

Science Process Skill

Guided Prediction

Science Concept

Liquids have no fixed shape but do have a fixed volume.

CONNECTIONS

 TO LANGUAGE

Discovery Chart—The children's shared predictions and discoveries about the capacity of several containers are recorded on a class chart.

 TO MATHEMATICS

Charting and Classifying—The children record their predictions and findings on charts.

Comparing—The children use comparative terms such as *more*, *less*, and *equal*. They may also use the mathematical symbols <, >, and =.

Science Vocabulary

compare
graph
liquid
more, less, equal
measure, measurement
shape
volume

Before the Activity

Prepare sets of containers by labeling each container with a different letter (A, B, C, . . .). Label identical containers, such as baby food jars, with the same letter. Fill an identical cup with water for each Discovery Group. You may wish to mark the water level with a permanent marker a few centimeters below the top of the cups to allow the children to measure and to help prevent spillage.

Prepare a Discovery Chart with three columns and title the chart "Water Levels."

Materials

water and towels

identical clear plastic cups

clear, labeled containers in various shapes and sizes *(5 or 6 per group)*

funnels

permanent marker *(optional)*

chart paper and markers

crayons or colored markers

"Less, More, or Equal" Discovery Page *(optional; see page 71; symbols may be covered before copying)*

What to Do

1. Show the children one of the cups of water and one of the empty containers. Ask, "Do you think this container will hold more water than I have in my cup? Less water? The same amount?" Hold a vote, and record the letter of the

container and the results of the vote in the "What We Predict" column on the Discovery Chart. Repeat the process with three or four other containers.

Water Levels		
Container	What We Predict	What We Found
A	more	more
B	less	
C	more	
D	the same	

2. With the class, test the predictions by pouring the water from the cup into each container. Ask, "Were our predictions correct? What should we write in the 'What We Found' column?" Talk with the children about their predictions and the outcomes.

THE LANGUAGE OF MATH

This activity gives you an opportunity to introduce one of the shorthand tools of science and mathematics. Symbols such as <, >, and = save time and space. Some children will pick up and use symbolic language quickly; other may need more time to become comfortable with it. Introduce such notation when you think the children are ready.

36 Discovery Science

3. Give each Discovery Group a plastic cup filled with water. Say, "I'm giving each group an identical cup filled with the same amount of water so that we can all compare how much water these containers hold in the same way. Later, we will talk about what we discovered."

4. Give each group five or six containers. They are to investigate which containers hold about 1 cup of water and which hold more or hold less. Say, "Look at your group's containers, and decide whether each container belongs in the Less, More, or Equal group." Have them record their predictions in their Discovery Journals or on the "Less, More, or Equal" Discovery Page.

5. Have each group test their predictions and record the results.

	Predict	Found
Baby food jar	less	less
Big cup	more	

6. Ask the groups to trade containers and repeat the process. Help groups compare their findings. Ask, "Did you get the same results as the other group?" If not, help them find out why.

Assessing the Activity

Do the children understand that different containers can hold the same amount of water? Hold up another container, and ask whether it will hold the same, more, or less water than the cup. Can the children justify their predictions? Can they group several containers according to their predictions?

Additional Stimulation

How Many?—Encourage the children to continue to explore the materials by giving them sentence frames to complete. For example, It takes _____ to fill _____ might be completed to read, *It takes 8 blue cups to fill the green bucket.*

Oops, Too Much!—Bring in some new and unusually shaped containers, and hold a class vote in which each child predicts how many cups of water each container will hold. To test the predictions, pour in the number of cups of water given by the smallest prediction, and continue to add water up to the largest prediction—then pour in any overpredicted amount of water until the container overflows: too much!

ACTIVITY 4

Water and a Little More

This is the first activity that gives the children experiences with liquids other than plain water. They will discover that solutions of sugar water and salt water do not always behave exactly like water. In the process, they will make some interesting observations.

CONNECTIONS

TO LANGUAGE

Expressive Language—The children expand their science vocabulary as they use words related to making solutions.

Discovery Journals—The children draw and write about their observations in their journals.

TO MATHEMATICS

Measuring—The children record the amount of salt and sugar they use to make their solutions.

Comparing—Through observation and discussion, the children compare the rate of dispersal of food coloring in salt water, sugar water, and plain water.

What to Do

1. Have the children work in pairs or Discovery Groups. Give each group three cups of water and a spoon. Each group will prepare a cup of salt water, a cup of sugar water, and leave the third cup plain water. Explain how to make the solutions: "Stir in the salt (or sugar), one spoonful at a time, until no more will dissolve in the water." (When no more will dissolve, a solution is called *saturated*.) Have the children record the number of spoonfuls they use to make the salt and the sugar solutions. Warn them to be careful to put the salt and the sugar in the correct cups.

2. Have groups place their cups where they will be visible but undisturbed, and then ask them to put one drop of food coloring in each cup and watch what happens (don't stir the water). After a few minutes, have them draw what they see in

---

Science Process Skill

Focused Observation

Science Concept

Many different liquids exist in the world.

Science Vocabulary

dissolve

liquid

mixture

saturated

solution

Materials

water and towels

food coloring

labeled containers of salt and sugar

clear plastic cups *(3 per group; label each set with the words* Sugar, Salt, *and* Water*)*

plastic spoons

Activity 4 **Water and a Little More** 39

their Discovery Journals, stopping periodically to observe. The coloring in the cup of water will disperse quickly; in the salt and sugar water, it will take up to several days.

3. Encourage the children to observe the cups in 1-hour intervals throughout the day. At the end of the day, have them draw and write about their observations. If possible, allow them to contribute their observations the next day.

4. Talk with the class about their observations. Encourage them to compare their findings with each other. Ask, "Do all our groups have the same results? Do the different colors react the same way? How does the food coloring in plain water act differently from food coloring in salt and sugar solutions?"

Assessing the Activity

Do the children's journal entries indicate differences in the dispersal rate of the food coloring in the different liquids? Do they effectively communicate their observations?

Additional Stimulation

Fun Stuff—Empty a box or two of cornstarch into a dishpan, and add enough water to make a thick liquid. It should be wet enough to drip from your fingers but dry enough to roll into a ball. The ball will "melt" as soon as you stop rolling; experiment until you find the right consistency. Let the children play with the substance, then make a Discovery Chart about its properties and how it is similar to and different from water. *(Do not dispose of this substance in a sink—it will clog the drain!)*

AMAZING LIQUIDS

All liquids have the shape and volume properties explored in the first three activities, but some liquids also have unique chemical and physical properties. For example:
- Oils will not mix with water.
- Alcohol evaporates quickly.
- Molten wax solidifies at room temperature.
- Mercury, a metal, melts far below room temperature.
- Bromine, a very poisonous liquid, vaporizes at room temperature.

Making Crystals—Have the children tie a string to the center of a craft stick and place the stick across a cup with the string suspended in a saturated salt or sugar solution. Also prepare a few cups without a string for comparison. As the water evaporates, the sugar or salt will form crystals on the string. On the cups without the string, crystals will form on the sides and bottom as the water evaporates. Talk with the children about the similarities and differences in the crystal formations.

Weird Stuff—Mix a small amount of water and cornstarch in a clear container, and let the children observe it until the cornstarch settles to the bottom. Talk about how this solution is different from the salt and sugar water: the cornstarch will not dissolve as salt and sugar do. The children can also experiment with trying to dissolve flour, baking soda, and baking powder in water.

MIXTURES AND SOLUTIONS

Because of its dissolving properties, water is called the universal solvent. We use water, for example, to put many food additives into a liquid form. When a solid dissolves in a liquid, the solid separates into the smallest particles possible and then mixes evenly with the liquid's molecules.

When we combine two or more substances, such as sand and salt, we create a mixture. Combining salt and water also creates a mixture—but a special type of mixture called a solution. In a *solution,* one substance (the solute—in this case, salt) is so well combined with the other (the solvent—in this case, water) that we can't see the separate materials.

We can separate a solution by the process of *evaporation.* When the solvent evaporates, it leaves the solute behind. Because we can recover the materials without using a chemical change, we know that the solution process is a physical change and not a chemical reaction.

ACTIVITY 5

Stick with Water

One of the most interesting things about water is its ability to stick to itself and to other things. Imagine a freshly washed automobile or a clean glass as it dries: the water sticks to the clean surface and forms beads. These examples tell us of two characteristics of water that we will explore in this activity. We call the ability of water to stick to itself *cohesion* and the ability of it to stick to other things *adhesion*.

CONNECTIONS

TO LANGUAGE

Discovery Chart—The children's shared discoveries about water's cohesive and adhesive properties are recorded on a class chart.

Discovery Journals—The children record their observations in their journals.

TO MATHEMATICS

Counting—The children count the number of drops of water they can place on a penny and the number of pennies they place in a cup of water before the water overflows.

TO THE FAMILY

This activity gives the children an opportunity to show their families what they have just discovered about some of the unique properties of liquids. Send home a note with the children, along with an eyedropper:

Your child has been learning many things about liquids. We'd like you and your child to investigate the ability of water to stick to itself and to other things. The ability of water to stick to itself is called cohesion. Let your child lead you and other family members through this activity. You will be asked to guess how many drops of water can be dropped onto a penny before the water overflows onto the table. Fill the eyedropper with water, and count the drops as you put them on the penny. How close were your guesses?

Science Process Skill

Focused Observation

Science Concept

Water is the most common liquid on earth.

Science Vocabulary

adhesion

cohesion

H_2O

Materials

water and towels

sheets of waxed paper *(1 per group)*

eyedroppers *(1 per group)*

chart paper and markers

graph paper

pennies *(about 25 per group)*

medicine cups *(the 30-ml or 1-oz cups used to dispense medicine)*

42 Discovery Science

What to Do

1. Give each Discovery Group a sheet of waxed paper and an eyedropper, and ask them to place drops of water on the waxed paper. Ask, "How does the water act on this surface? What is the shape of a drop?" Have them draw the shape of a water drop from the top and from the side in their Discovery Journals.

2. Ask, "Does the size of the drop make a difference—do drops of different sizes have different shapes? How big can a drop be? Try to make the biggest drop you can on the waxed paper." Next, ask, "Does water stick together? What happens when you lift the waxed paper until the water runs off?"

3. Give each group a penny, and ask them to put as many drops of water on the coin as possible. Say, "Count the drops as you go. Do it again! How many drops does your penny hold? Write down this number. Did some groups get more drops than others?" Have the children draw—from the top and from the side—the penny and the water drop that formed on it. Talk with them about the idea that water can stick together and form a shape.

Activity 5 **Stick with Water** 43

4. Give each group a medicine cup and 20 to 30 pennies. Have them fill the cup with water to the top and then, very carefully, drop a penny in the water. Ask, "Did the water run over?" (If they are careful, it won't.) "Why didn't it run over?" In the discussion, help the children understand that the water didn't run over because water sticks to itself and to the sides of the cup. The cup will hold many coins before the water overflows. Have the children guess how many coins they think the cup will hold before the water spills over the edge. Again, have them experiment, observe, and then draw the shape of the surface of the water.

5. Review each of the activities the children have completed, focusing on the properties of adhesion and cohesion. A liquid (in this case, water) sticks to waxed paper and to many other surfaces (adhesion), especially clean surfaces. It makes the same shape each time. This shape is its response to sticking to itself (cohesion) and to the surface. Record and summarize the children's findings on a Discovery Chart. Encourage them to define and use the vocabulary words.

How We Know Water Sticks to Itself "cohesion"	How We Know Water Sticks to Other Things "adhesion"
1.	1.
2.	2.

Assessing the Activity

Can the children describe all of the properties of water that they have observed?

Additional Stimulation

Try It Again—Give the children another liquid—such as honey, glycerin, or syrup—and have them repeat any of the activities they did with water. Ask, "Do these liquids act like water? How do they differ?"

Slick Water—Add some detergent to water, and have them repeat the activities and talk about the results.

Sinkers—Let the children try filling floating containers until they sink. For example, ask how many drops of water will fit in a bottle cap before it will sink.

ACTIVITY 6

How Many Drops Till It Drips?

All children are familiar with spills and the cleanup that follows. Which brand of paper towel works best to soak up spilled liquid? In this activity the children get a chance to test and identify the most absorbent products. They can also share their new consumer information with their families.

CONNECTIONS

 TO LANGUAGE

Written Language—The children label paper towels by brand name.

 TO MATHEMATICS

Counting—The children count the drops of water each towel absorbs.

Graphing—The children make bar graphs to compare the absorbency of paper towels.

Before the Activity

Collect samples of different brands of paper towels. You might send a note home explaining the activity and how the results will be shared. Each child can bring in one paper towel sheet with the brand written on the sheet.

You may want to cut out the paper towel pieces yourself so they are all the same size. Place them in a container with the brand name and any available advertising for that brand. Alternatively, have the children trace around templates to cut out uniform pieces.

Decide whether you want the children to make individual graphs or each Discovery Group to create its own graph.

Science Process Skill

Observing to Classify

Science Concept

Water is the most common liquid on earth.

Science Vocabulary

absorb, absorbent
saturate
soak

Materials

water and towels

chart paper and markers *(optional)*

single sheets of paper towels from a variety of brands used at home and school

2 cm × 10 cm cardboard rectangles *(1 per group to use as a tracing template)*

scissors

string

tape

eyedroppers

containers to hold water

"How Many Drops?" Discovery Page *(optional; see page 72)*

interlocking cubes *(optional)*

---

46 Discovery Science

What to Do

1. On a Discovery Chart or on the board, make a list with the children of all the brands of paper towels the class has collected, including the towels your school uses. Talk as a group about the claims television commercials make about specific brands of paper towels. Ask, "Do you think the paper towels you use at home work better than the ones in our school bathroom? Let's find out!"

2. Have each Discovery Group make a "clothesline" by stretching a length of string between two chairs and tying or taping it in place.

3. Next, have each group select a rectangle of each paper towel brand and write the name of the brand on each sample in pencil. (The number of brands you have available will determine whether groups test all of the brands or just a few. Ideally, each group will test at least five or six brands.) The children then fold the rectangles in half and hang them on the clothesline. Have them list the names of the towels they are testing in their Discovery Journals or on the "How Many Drops?" Discovery Page.

4. Say, "Use the dropper to put water on a towel strip one drop at a time." (They may need a bit of practice to control the water drops. Caution them to wait between drops so the water moves down the paper strip; too many drops too quickly will produce inaccurately high counts.) "Count each drop, and stop when water begins to drip from your strip. Write the number of drops next to that brand name in your journals. Keep going until you have added water to all your towel strips."

Activity 6 **How Many Drops Till It Drips?** 47

5. When groups have tested all their strips, have each group list the towels in order from the one that held the fewest drops to the one that held the most. Have each group make a bar graph (in their Discovery Journals or on the Discovery Page) of the number of drops of water each brand held. You may want them to create a bar graph with interlocking cubes instead, using a different color for each brand.

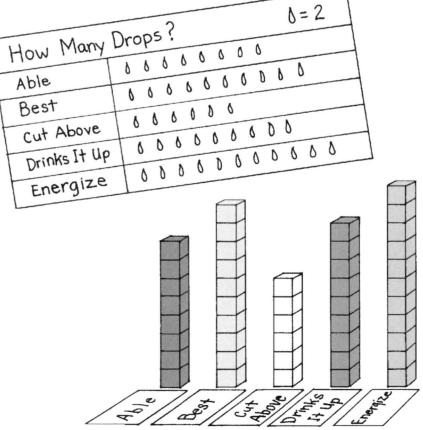

6. Have the groups compare their results by looking at each other's graphs. Talk about whether a certain brand is a clear winner or loser, and about the possible reasons some towels absorb more water than others. Make a class graph recording the drops of water for each brand.

Number of Drops

Brand	Group 1	Group 2	Group 3	Total
Able	16	18	12	46
Best				

Assessing the Activity

Can the children identify which towel in their group absorbs the most water? Are they able to describe the procedure they used and why it was done this way?

Additional Stimulation

Let's Do It Some More—Let the children test other materials—newsprint, toilet tissue, wrapping paper, or fabrics—and compare absorbency. Ask, "Would our test results be the same if we used different liquids?" Try syrup or honey.

How Do You Hang?—Have the children try hanging the towels in different positions—perhaps from one corner with a paper clip or folded in half lengthwise. Talk about any effect this has on the number of drops the towels absorb.

Brainstorm—Have the children list all of the ways paper towels can be used. Ask questions to challenge them to be creative as they develop their list. "Can you think of a way you might use a paper towel as a toy? How could you use a paper towel outdoors?"

Activity 6 **How Many Drops Till It Drips?** 49

ACTIVITY 7

Which Drop Hangs Around Longest?

The liquids observed by the children in this activity will have a variety of densities and consistencies. By experimenting with the various liquids, the children should soon learn to predict which kinds of liquids—based on their characteristics—will evaporate more rapidly than others.

CONNECTIONS

 TO LANGUAGE

Discovery Journals—The children record their observations in their journals.

Written Language—The children label paper towels with the names of the liquids they are testing. Then, they record their observations about how much time each liquid took to evaporate.

 TO MATHEMATICS

Time—The children discuss the amount of time various liquids take to evaporate.

What to Do

1. Distribute the paper towel squares to the Discovery Groups. Ask each group to choose six of the various liquids to test, including water.

2. Have them write the name of each liquid on a paper towel square, place two drops of each liquid on the corresponding towel square, and lay the towel squares flat on the drying racks. Note the time or set the timer.

3. Talk with the children about the liquids they used and what they observed as they placed them on the towels. Help them to record the name of each liquid and to draw a picture or describe the liquids in their Discovery Journals or on the "Evaporate!" Discovery Page.

Science Process Skill
Focused Observation

Science Concept
Many different liquids exist in the world.

Science Vocabulary
evaporate

liquid names

Materials
water and towels

several other liquids, such as vinegar, honey, water, ketchup, liquid glue, liquid starch, and tempera paint *(clearly label each container)*

5-cm squares of paper towels *(4–6 per group)*

"Evaporate!" Discovery Page *(optional; see page 73)*

drying racks or trays

eyedroppers

clock or timer

50 Discovery Science

EVAPORATION

Evaporation is the process by which liquids change to gases. The molecules at the surface of a liquid move into the air as water vapor or other airborne compounds. The greater the liquid's surface area, the more space in which this movement can occur. Liquids that are spread over large areas have a greater surface for the exchange.

4. Have the children observe the liquids on the towels periodically and record their observations of which have evaporated and at what time. Some will evaporate quickly—in just a few seconds or minutes. Others will need to be checked every 15 minutes or so, as they will evaporate more slowly.

5. Discuss how the different liquids evaporated. Ask, "Did the liquids evaporate at the same speed? Did some evaporate very quickly and others take several days?"

Activity 7 **Which Drop Hangs Around Longest?** 51

Assessing the Activity

Do the children recognize that different liquids evaporate at different rates?

Additional Stimulation

Let's Try Some More!—Encourage the children to think of other liquids they could test. Let them try them if possible.

Evaporation Around Us—Have the children talk about examples of evaporation in their daily lives—for example, clothes drying, snow melting and evaporating, dew on plants evaporating, paintings drying, and puddles disappearing.

ACTIVITY 8

Look Closer

By this age, most children have explored magnifying glasses and know that they make objects appear larger. Some of the children may wear glasses—or have tried on someone else's glasses—and know that the lenses change how the world appears. This activity lets the children discover the natural magnifying qualities of water.

CONNECTIONS

TO LANGUAGE

Expressive Language—Children use comparative language as they talk about magnification.

TO MATHEMATICS

Comparing—Children test and compare the magnifying effect of different sizes of drops of water.

TO THE FAMILY

Children can surprise their families with a simple homemade magnifier. Put an eyedropper, a 10-centimeter square of waxed paper, and a 10-centimeter square of newspaper in a resealable plastic bag for each child, and send the items home with this note:

We'd like you and your child to work together to discover the natural magnifying qualities of water. Place the square of newspaper on a table, and cover it with the square of waxed paper. Put one drop of water on the waxed paper. What happens to the writing that you see through the water? Add more water to the drop. How does the print change? Try to find the amount of water that magnifies the newsprint the best.

Before the Activity

Cut an opening in the side of the plastic bucket. Cover the top of the bucket with plastic wrap and hold it in place with a rubber band. (You may want to make a bucket apparatus for each group.)

Science Process Skill

Focused Observation

Science Concept

Water is the most common liquid on earth.

Science Vocabulary

compare

larger, smaller

magnify, magnification

Materials

water and towels

eyedroppers *(1 per child or group)*

10-cm squares of waxed paper

10-cm squares of newspaper, magazine pages, or any other printed material

half-gallon plastic bucket *(such as an ice-cream tub or fast-food-chicken bucket)*

plastic wrap

large rubber band

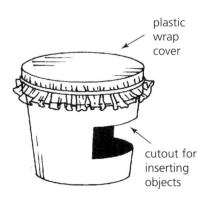

What to Do

1. Give each child or Discovery Group an eyedropper, a square of waxed paper, and a square of printed material. Have them place the printed material under the waxed paper.

2. Say, "Put one drop of water on the waxed paper. What happens to the writing you see through the water?" Talk with the children about what they see, and ask them to draw the setup in their Discovery Journals.

3. Have the children add more water to the drop and talk about how the print changes. Ask, "Can you find the best way to magnify the print?"

4. Show the children the bucket apparatus. Let them place objects in the hole and look at them through the plastic-wrap cover. Talk about what they see.

5. Have the children pour a small amount of water on the cover. Ask, "What do you see now?" Let them experiment to find what amount of water makes the best magnifier. Have them draw the apparatus in their Discovery Journals and write about what they saw (what they write will vary with their skill and experience).

Assessing the Activity

Do the children realize that there is an amount of water that is just right to magnify—that too much or too little water doesn't work as well?

Additional Stimulation

Let's Experiment—Encourage the children to experiment with and compare other liquids (such as vinegar, clear corn syrup, sugar water, and salt water) or containers of other sizes.

All Kinds of Magnifiers—Provide an assortment of magnifiers, and let the children investigate their magnification abilities. Compare the commercial magnifiers to those the children made. Are they clearer? Do they magnify better? Are they easier to use? Why?

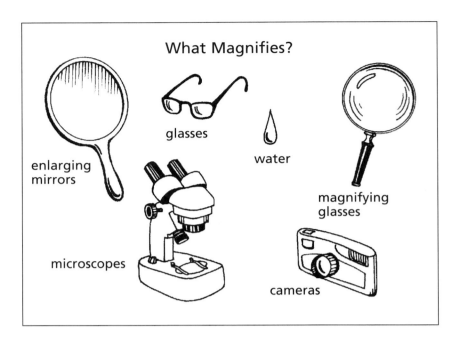

What Else Magnifies?—Have the children brainstorm all the things they know about that make objects look bigger. You can all bring items into class to share. You may want to invite people who use magnifiers in their occupation to visit the class and talk about the tools and their uses.

ACTIVITY 9

Water Clocks

The rate at which water will flow from one container to another is fairly uniform, and this consistency has been used for centuries to measure time. This activity challenges children to design and calibrate their own version of this ancient clock.

CONNECTIONS

 TO LANGUAGE

Discovery Chart—The children's shared discoveries about the construction and operation of water clocks are recorded on a class chart.

Expressive Language—The children use comparative language as they talk about the rate of flow in the water clocks.

 TO MATHEMATICS

Time—The children measure the amount of time it takes for their water clocks to empty.

Graphing—The children create graphs to compare the run times of various water clocks.

Before the Activity

Make some simple water clocks. To make a water clock, use a nail to punch a hole in the bottom of a cup. Vary the size of the cup and the size of the hole. You may also make them from cans and plastic cups, but wrap duct tape around the edges of cans so no one gets cut! For plastic cups, heat the nail to melt a hole. Check that the hole in each container allows water to run out in 60 seconds or less.

Play around with the clocks to create one that empties in 10 to 15 seconds when a fixed amount of water is poured into it. Indicate the water level for this cup with a permanent marker.

Each Discovery Group will need about four water clocks. Label each clock with a numeral or letter so they can be identified on a chart. Create five or six of one clock so that each group will have one identical clock. Label each of the identical clocks with a star.

Science Process Skill
Organizing and Communicating Observations

Science Concept
Water is the most common liquid on earth.

Science Vocabulary
graph
timer
water clock

Materials
water and towels

paper cups of various sizes

nails of various sizes

large clock with second hand

containers to collect draining water *(1 per group)*

permanent marker

"Water Clock Data" Discovery Page *(optional; see page 74)*

Activity 9 **Water Clocks** 57

What to Do

1. Show the children the water clocks. Say, "These are water clocks. Every time we pour a specific amount of water into one of these clocks, it takes the same amount of time for the water to run out." Show them the water clock you have timed. Pour in the predetermined amount of water while your finger is covering the hole. Explain how to time the water clock using the second hand of the large clock. Release your finger, and have the children time the water clock. Record the seconds on a Discovery Chart. Repeat the process. Ask, "Did we get the same time? What do you think will happen if we put in less water?" Write their response on the Discovery Chart. Try it, and record the outcome.

2. Give each group one of the star clocks and three other water clocks. Each group will also need water and a container for the draining water.

3. Let them investigate, listing the clocks in their Discovery Journals or on the "Water Clock Data" Discovery Page according to their labels and recording the times they measure. After ample time for exploration, reassemble as a group.

58 Discovery Science

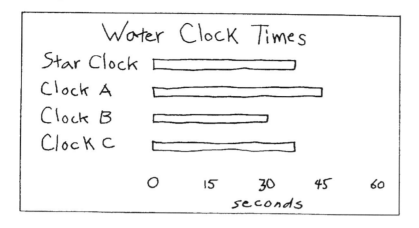

4. Ask, "What makes a difference in how long a water clock runs?" Write the children's ideas on the Discovery Chart. Talk about the effect of the size of the hole in the cup, the size of the container, and the amount of water used.

5. Discuss the fact that every group had one clock that was the same. Write the time each group recorded for the star clock on the Discovery Chart. Ask, "Why aren't these times the same? What could we do that might make them the same?" Help the children agree on a fixed amount of water to place in the star clocks, and have them try it and time them. List the times. There may be minor differences; talk about the fact that these are homemade timers and are not as accurate as something that is precisely built.

Assessing the Activity

Do the children understand that the more water that is used, the longer a particular clock runs?

Additional Stimulation

Let's Do Some More—Give the children a variety of cups, cans, and nails, and let them create their own water clocks (make sure they are careful with the nails). Encourage them to experiment with holes in various places and of various sizes. Ask, "Can you make two clocks that look different but run for the same length of time?"

Better Clocks—Tell the children there is a way to time their clocks more precisely. Give each group a 30-ml plastic cup (a medicine cup), and say, "I want you to use this little cup to measure the water to time your clocks. Time a clock with 1 cup, and then with 2, 3, and 4 cups of water." (You may want to talk about a specific number of milliliters instead of "cups.")

Show them how to record the information on a bar graph in their Discovery Journals or on the "Water Clock Data" Discovery Page. Have them time their star clock and two other clocks and graph the results. Ask, "Did everyone get about the same results for their star clocks? Which clock runs the fastest? Which runs the slowest?"

Talk about the graphs and their similarities. "What happens to the time of a water clock when we add more water?" Record the question and the children's responses on the Discovery Chart. You may want to have the groups trade clocks and see whether they get the same results.

Water Clock Mania—Place a length of wooden dowel in a fixed upright position (a standard plunger works well for this). Show the children how water clocks made from paper cups can be attached to the dowel with pushpins so that water drains from one into another. Mention that the hole doesn't have to be in the center of the bottom of the cups; they could punch them near the edge or on the side instead. Challenge them to arrange a series of clocks so that the water makes its way from top to bottom. Clocks could also be attached to the center pole on an artificial tree, to hooks on pegboard, to plywood, or to anything else you have available.

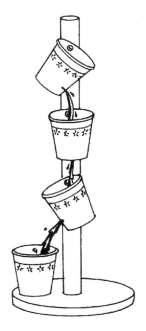

60 Discovery Science

Mystery Clock—Place a water clock and three graphs you have made in the Discovery Center. Challenge the children to play with the clock to figure out which graph belongs to the Mystery Clock.

Frozen Water Clocks—Freeze water in a cup the same size as one of the water clocks. Have the children time this clock. Talk with them about their observations.

A Library of Clocks—Hang up pictures of clocks and read books on clocks to the children. The encyclopedia will probably have a good section on clocks and may describe water clocks.

ACTIVITY 10

Through Thick and Thin

Objects move though liquids in different ways. This activity allows the children to explore the properties of a variety of liquids by observing how objects move in them.

CONNECTIONS

 TO LANGUAGE

Expressive Language—The children use descriptive vocabulary as they share their findings.

Discovery Chart—The children's shared discoveries about the rate at which different objects fall through various liquids are recorded on a class chart.

 TO MATHEMATICS

Comparing—The children compare the time it takes for objects to move through different liquids.

Before the Activity

Send home a note asking families to send in clear bottles and jars with lids. Prepare two or three bottles with a liquid and a few objects each, and label them with the name of the liquid. To prepare the sugar syrup, mix equal amounts of water and sugar and boil the mixture until it thickens.

sugar syrup

water

salad oil

Science Process Skill
Guided Inference

Science Concept
Many different liquids exist in the world.

Science Vocabulary
dense, density

descriptive words such as thicker, slowly, runny, watery, and quickly

float

liquid

liquid names

sink

Materials
water and towels

other liquids, such as vinegar, carbonated water, honey, mineral oil, salad oil, motor oil, liquid detergent, corn syrup, and sugar syrup

clear bottles and jars with tight lids, such as spice jars, beverage bottles, salad dressing bottles, and peanut butter jars

small objects, such as beads, stones, sequins, marbles, paper clips, and metal and rubber washers

funnels

62 Discovery Science

What to Do

1. Display the bottles you have prepared. As you invert the bottles, encourage the children to compare the liquids and the rate at which the objects move through them.

2. Say, "Now you will each make your own bottle." Let each child choose a liquid, fill a container (using funnels if needed), and choose two or three items to place in the container. Have them drop the items into the liquids.

3. Ask them to put the lids on very tightly, turn the bottles over, and see what happens. Say, "Show each other your bottles. Can you find one in which the objects move faster than yours and another in which the objects move slower? You may not be able to find both." Encourage the children to talk about their observations with each other and to make comparisons.

Activity 10 **Through Thick and Thin** 63

4. Make a Discovery Chart with the children. Help them come up with a rule about how objects move in different liquids. Encourage them to think of as many ways as possible to describe differences in the liquids and in the objects as they move.

How Things Move in Liquid

In Water
- fast, straight down
- easy

In Corn Syrup

In Oil
- slowly, takes time

In Honey

Assessing the Activity

Are the children able to compare the ways the objects move in different liquids?

Additional Stimulation

Try Some More—Ask the children to suggest other liquids to compare and predict what will happen. Allow them to test their predictions if possible.

Order the Liquids—Ask the children to put the containers in order from slowest- to fastest-dropping (or rising) objects.

The Magic Pool—Have the children imagine that they have a magic swimming pool: all they have to do is touch a magic button, and the water will change to whatever liquid they desire! Let each child choose a liquid and draw and write about how it would affect their play in the magic swimming pool. A variation on this is to have the children imagine playing in the rain—with other liquids falling from the clouds instead of water.

ACTIVITY 11

Will It Freeze?

This activity will help the children construct an understanding of another characteristic of liquids. They have already observed that water freezes. In this activity they explore what happens to other liquids when they become very cold. When placed in a freezer, some liquids will become denser but will not freeze.

CONNECTIONS

 TO LANGUAGE

Expressive Language—The children use descriptive language to describe the different liquids and how they change throughout the activity.

Discovery Chart—The children's shared descriptions of the liquids and discoveries about whether the liquids freeze are recorded on a class chart.

 TO MATHEMATICS

Predicting—Based on their experiences with water, the children predict what will happen to other liquids placed in a freezer.

Comparing—The children compare their predictions to what actually occurs.

Before the Activity

Mark the 15-ml level on each medicine cup with a permanent marker. Attach one of the labels, which are numbered from 1 to 15, to each cup. Each Discovery Group will have a number and a different liquid to test.

What to Do

1. Give each child an ice cube, and ask what they know about ice. As they watch the ice melt, make a list of their ideas and observations on a Discovery Chart. Say, "Ice is a form of water that is very cold. Some substances change when they are placed in a freezer. Water changes into ice. Let's see what happens to other liquids we put in the freezer."

Science Process Skill
Guided Prediction

Science Concept
Many different liquids exist in the world.

Science Vocabulary
freeze
liquid names
melt
predict
result
solid, solidify
test

Materials
various liquids such as water, glycerin, liquid starch, shampoo, fabric softener, coffee, soft drinks, liquid glue, liquid detergent, motor oil, ketchup, milk, honey, and cooking oil *(1 per group; all should be labeled and safe to touch)*

towels

medicine cups *(1 per group)*

permanent marker

ice cubes

freezer

tray for placing filled cups in the freezer

liquid labels *(see page 75)*

tape

Activity 11 **Will It Freeze?** 65

LIQUID METAL

Iron is a solid at room temperature. When iron is heated to several thousand degrees, the molecules are active enough that the substance changes to its liquid phase. Pour it into a mold and, like all liquids, it takes on the shape of the container. Let it cool, and it will solidify.

2. Give each Discovery Group a different liquid. Say, "Smell your liquid—*but don't taste it!* Feel it. How is it like water? How is it different?" Have them record their impressions in their Discovery Journals. Give each group one of the marked cups, and have them fill it to the line with their liquid. Help them write the name of the liquid on the label.

3. Have the class discuss how each liquid looks, feels, and smells, and what they observed as they poured the liquid into the cups. Record the descriptions on the Discovery Chart under the name of the liquid. Beginning with water, have the groups predict what will happen to their liquid in the freezer. Help them to carefully circle their prediction on the label. Have the children place all the cups on the tray, and place the tray in the freezer.

Our Liquid Tests						
Liquid	Looks	Feels	Smells	Predict: Will it Freeze?	Test: Did it Freeze?
1. water	clear	plain	nothing	yes	
2. oil	fuzzy	slippery	weird	no	
3. milk	white	milky	nothing	yes	
4. honey	golden	sticky	sweet	yes	

66 Discovery Science

THE EFFECT OF SALT

The salt content of a liquid greatly affects whether it will freeze. Generally speaking, the more salt in a liquid, the lower its freezing point. The freezing points of many common liquids, such as ketchup, is well below the freezing point of most home freezers.

4. The next day, remove the cups of liquids from the freezer and redistribute them to the groups. Encourage the children to look at and touch their sample. Ask, "Did all the liquids freeze like water does?" Encourage them to discuss how the different liquids reacted to being in the freezer and to compare what actually happened to what they expected. Record their observations on the Discovery Chart. Have the groups put all their samples together so everyone can observe them.

5. Have the children observe the substances as they warm to room temperature. Ask, "Do some substances return to liquid faster than others?"

Activity 11 **Will It Freeze?** 67

Assessing the Activity

Can the children talk about the differences between liquids? Do they observe that liquids act differently when they are cooled?

Additional Stimulation

Freezing More Fluids—Have the children repeat the activity with different liquids. Encourage them to think of their own liquids to try.

Salt and Ice—Have the children make salt solutions in varying concentrations, labeling the containers with the number of spoonfuls of salt they used. After the containers have been in the freezer overnight, have the children inspect whether the amount of salt in water affects how it freezes.

Ice Cream—Using your own ice cream recipe, fruit juice, or commercial chocolate milk (it has a nice, creamy consistency), let the children freeze a snack. Put the liquid inside a tightly sealed container, place it in a large coffee can, pack ice and salt around it, and have the children roll and shake the can until the liquid is softly frozen. Another option is to pour the liquid into a quart-size resealable bag, then place that bag in a gallon-size resealable bag (heavy-duty freezer bags work well) containing ice and a few tablespoons of salt. Seal the large bag, and have the children gently squish the bags until the liquid freezes to their satisfaction.

68 Discovery Science

CHECKPOINT ACTIVITY

Shape Changing

The children have explored many kind of liquids and many properties of liquids. As a final activity, you will again assess their understanding of the concept of the conservation of volume.

CONNECTIONS

 TO LANGUAGE

Expressive Language—The children use their own language and level of conceptualization to make operational definitions for the physical characteristics of liquids as they respond to the container being manipulated.

 TO MATHEMATICS

Conservation of Volume—The children develop their own conceptual explanations for this important phenomenon.

Before the Activity

This activity is best done in a small-group discussion format. You may want to give some thought as to which children you would like to have in each Discovery Group, as this is an opportunity to dialogue with them and observe where they are in their concept attainment. Some combinations of group members could leave some children way behind others.

Before they begin, help the children review the Discovery Charts and their Discovery Journals. Talk with them about the activities they have done in the unit.

What to Do

1. Display the plastic bottle completely filled with lightly colored water. Ask, "What will happen if I squeeze the sides of this bottle?" Hopefully, someone will predict that the water will run out. If not, remind them to think about what happens when they squeeze a plastic ketchup or mustard bottle.

2. Squeeze the bottle as the children observe. Catch the overflow in a cup for later discussion. Now ask, "Why was the water forced out of the bottle?" Look for indications in their responses that the water spills out because the shape or size

Science Process Skill

Guided Prediction

Science Concept

Liquid has no definite shape but has a definite volume.

Science Vocabulary

overflow

volume

Materials

water *(lightly tint the water with food coloring)*

towels

small, clear plastic squeeze bottle

cup or bowl to catch the overflow

oil, vinegar, or another liquid

of the bottle has been changed. Do they state in their own words that water (a liquid) has a definite volume and that if there is not enough room in the bottle, some water must escape?

3. Screw the lid on the bottle to give the smashed bottle the appearance of being full. Ask the children whether the bottle is full. They should say yes, it is full because there is no air space in the bottle, only water. Can they state in their own words that water will take the shape of any container?

4. Loosen the lid, allowing air to enter the bottle, and ask whether the bottle is still full. The children should realize that it is not full since it is no longer filled with water.

5. Prepare to return the water from the overflow cup to the bottle, but before you do, ask, "What will the water level in the bottle be if all the water is poured back?" They should reply that the water will be at the level at which we began, full. If the bottle has not regained its full shape and some of the water doesn't fit, talk about this with the children.

6. Fill the bottle with a different liquid. Repeat the question-and-demonstration process, and determine whether the children have come to understand that all liquids behave similarly when there are changes in container size.

Assessing the Activity

The children will range widely in their understanding of volume relationships as they relate to the sequence of demonstrations and questions. Look for an initial indication of understanding in some children; others may offer much more complete and accurate accounts. Also, you may increase your expectations when you repeat the sequence of questions with a different liquid. The children's accuracy and clarity should improve noticeably the second time around.

Additional Stimulation

Get Precise—Have the children try a similar process, but use a graduated cylinder to quantify the amount of liquid in the plastic bottle. Ask, "How much is squeezed out, how much remains, and how much is there when all the water is measured together? Does it equal the original amount of water?"

Name

Less, More, or Equal

	What We Predict			
Container	< Less	> More	= Equal	What We Found
A				
B				
C				
D				
E				

© Dale Seymour Publications®

The Wonders of Water 71

Name _____

How Many Drops?

Number of Drops

24
22
20
18
16
14
12
10
8
6
4
2

_____ _____ _____ _____ _____ _____

72 Discovery Science

© Dale Seymour Publications®

Name _____

Evaporate!

Liquid: _____

Time to evaporate: _____

Liquid: _____

Time to evaporate: _____

Liquid: _____

Time to evaporate: _____

Liquid: _____

Time to evaporate: _____

Liquid: _____

Time to evaporate: _____

Liquid: _____

Time to evaporate: _____

© Dale Seymour Publications®

The Wonders of Water 73

Name _____

Water Clock Data

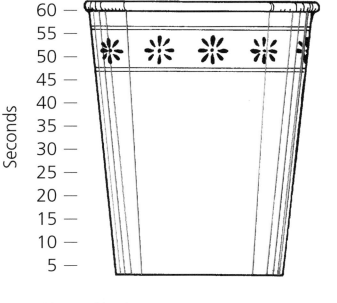

Seconds: 60, 55, 50, 45, 40, 35, 30, 25, 20, 15, 10, 5

Water Clock _____

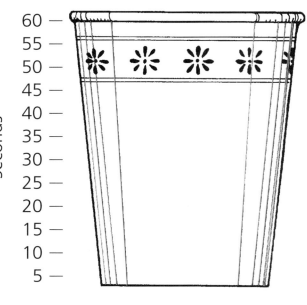

Seconds: 60, 55, 50, 45, 40, 35, 30, 25, 20, 15, 10, 5

Water Clock _____

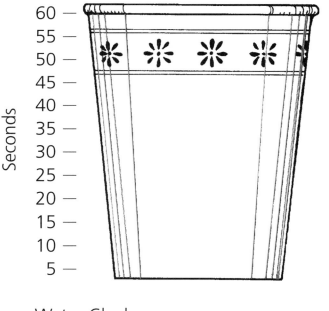

Seconds: 60, 55, 50, 45, 40, 35, 30, 25, 20, 15, 10, 5

Water Clock _____

Seconds: 60, 55, 50, 45, 40, 35, 30, 25, 20, 15, 10, 5

Water Clock _____

Liquid Labels

1 Liquid: _____ Will it freeze?　yes　no Did it freeze?　yes　no	**2** Liquid: _____ Will it freeze?　yes　no Did it freeze?　yes　no	**3** Liquid: _____ Will it freeze?　yes　no Did it freeze?　yes　no
4 Liquid: _____ Will it freeze?　yes　no Did it freeze?　yes　no	**5** Liquid: _____ Will it freeze?　yes　no Did it freeze?　yes　no	**6** Liquid: _____ Will it freeze?　yes　no Did it freeze?　yes　no
7 Liquid: _____ Will it freeze?　yes　no Did it freeze?　yes　no	**8** Liquid: _____ Will it freeze?　yes　no Did it freeze?　yes　no	**9** Liquid: _____ Will it freeze?　yes　no Did it freeze?　yes　no
10 Liquid: _____ Will it freeze?　yes　no Did it freeze?　yes　no	**11** Liquid: _____ Will it freeze?　yes　no Did it freeze?　yes　no	**12** Liquid: _____ Will it freeze?　yes　no Did it freeze?　yes　no
13 Liquid: _____ Will it freeze?　yes　no Did it freeze?　yes　no	**14** Liquid: _____ Will it freeze?　yes　no Did it freeze?　yes　no	**15** Liquid: _____ Will it freeze?　yes　no Did it freeze?　yes　no

Water Clip Art

76 Discovery Science © Dale Seymour Publications®